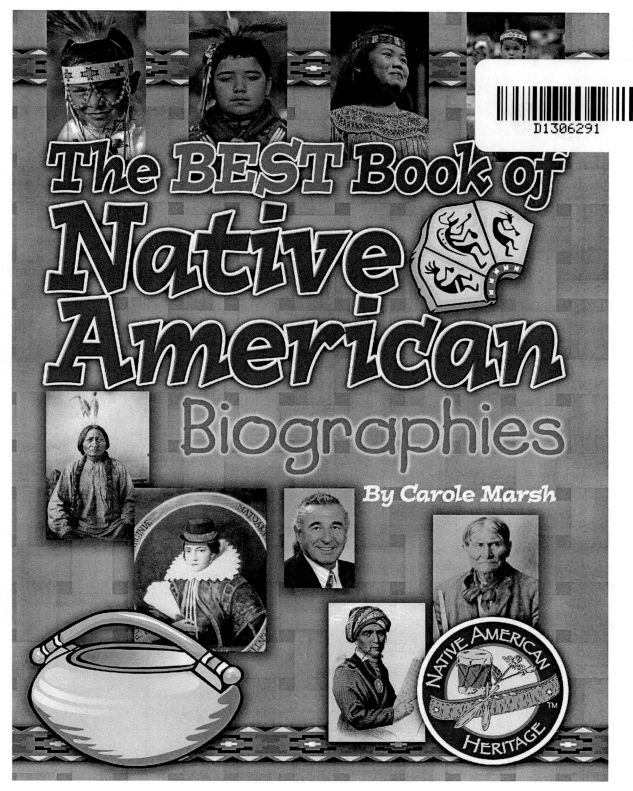

The BEST Book of Native American Biographies

By Carole Marsh

Editor: Jenny Corsey
Graphic Design & Layout: Cecil Anderson and Lynette Rowe
Cover Design: Victoria DeJoy

1

Published by

GALLOPADE™
INTERNATIONAL

800-536-2GET
www.gallopade.com

Gallopade is proud to be a member of these educational organizations and associations:

The National School Supply and Equipment Association (NSSEA)
National Association for Gifted Children (NAGC)
American Booksellers Association (ABA)
Association of Partners for Public Lands (APPL)
Museum Store Association (MSA)
Publishers Marketing Association (PMA)
International Reading Association (IRA)

Native American Heritage™ Series

The Big Book of Native American Activities

The Native American Heritage Coloring Book

Celebrating Native American Heritage: 20 Days of Activities, Reading, Recipes, Parties, Plays, and More!

Mini-Timeline of Awesome Native American Achievements and Events

State Indians: A Kid's Look at Our State's Chiefs, Tribes, Reservations, Powwows, Lore and More From the Past and the Present!

Available for all 50 states!

Native American Heritage Readers™

Black Hawk	Tecumseh	Sitting Bull
Chief Powhatan	Sacagawea	Geronimo
Pocahontas	Sequoyah	Crazy Horse
Ben Nighthorse Campbell		

African American Heritage Series: Black Jazz, Pizzazz, & Razzmatazz™
12 Exciting Products!

Hispanic Heritage Series: Fiesta! Siesta! & All the Resta!™
6 Exciting Products!

3

What is a biography, anyway? We usually think of it as the life story of someone famous. When someone has achieved a special goal, accomplished something significant in history, discovered something that will help mankind, or created a work of art—we want to know more about that person.

I think the best biographies are of the ordinary person. We may not even know their name, but their life can be fascinating to us. Everyone has a biography (even a kid!)—a life story of what has happened to them and what they have done up to this point. While you might think your biography is boring, it may be very exciting to someone who has lived an entirely different kind of life in a completely different type of place.

What can a kid learn from a biography? How other people have *had* to live their lives. And how they have *chosen* to live their lives. How everything you learn and do becomes part of the *you* that can often go on and do great things in spite of (and often because of!) a hard life, poverty, discrimination, handicaps, and other *negative* things that only <u>you</u> can turn to *positive*!

You can learn that we're all pretty special. We all have something important to do while we're here on Earth. We may not know exactly what that is. We may never even find out. But when we can look and see how others may also have thought they had little to contribute, but made a great difference, even in the life of one other person—we can have hope that what we do is important too.

In fact the most important biographies have never (and probably never will) be written. If they were, they would be the biographies of our grandparents, our mothers, our fathers, our brothers and sisters, our aunts and uncles, our special friends, the teachers who helped us, the employer who gave us our first job, even our beloved pets.

After you read this book about some famous and not so famous folks, I hope you will begin to look for biographies *everywhere*! In the newspaper, on television, in your schoolbooks, in letters, in conversations.

After all, biographies are not written all at once. They are written like our lives. One day at a time.

Carole Marsh

Many non-Indians have the idea that Native Americans are a "vanishing race." Nothing could be further from the truth! The Native American population throughout the continent is on the rise. In 1900, there were only about 400,000 Native Americans. Today, there are over 2,000,000 Native Americans living and prospering in the United States!

Native Americans, too, are working harder than ever to make sure their voices are heard. As more and more Native Americans are educated as lawyers, doctors, teachers, and journalists, they are finding new ways to fight discrimination and command respect for Indian beliefs and traditions.

American Indian and Alaska Native Fastest Growing Population
— U.S. Census Bureau

The American Indian and Alaska Native population is increasing faster than the population as a whole. In 1990, there were nearly 2 million American Indians and Alaska Natives. The number who declared themselves only American Indian or Alaska Native grew by more than 500,000 in 2000, or 26 percent. The number who declared themselves at least partially American Indian or Alaska Native in combination with other races grew by 2.2 million in 2000, an increase of 110 percent.

About 43 percent of all American Indians lived in the West, with 31 percent in the South. Among those who identified themselves as American Indian in the 2000 Census, 79 percent specified a particular tribe. The largest 6 tribes — Cherokee, Navajo, Latin American Indian, Choctaw, Sioux, and Chippewa — composed 40 percent of the American Indian and Alaska Native population. The Alaska Native tribe with the largest population was Eskimo.

"From Wakan Tanka, the Great Spirit, there came a great
unifying life force that flowed in and through all things …"
—Luther Standing Bear (Oglala, Lakota)

Dennis J. Banks co-founded the American Indian Movement (AIM) organization and served as the Director of the Sacred Run Foundation. He was a leader, teacher, lecturer, activist, and author.

Roberta Blackgoat, the Navajo "Fighting Grandmother," fought for two decades for the right to live on her homelands on sacred Big Mountain.

Ben Nighthorse Campbell, United States Senator

Ben Nighthorse Campbell's father was a Northern Cheyenne Indian, and his mother was of Portuguese descent. He served in the U.S. Air Force from 1951 to 1953. Campbell went to San Jose State University and also attended Meiji University in Tokyo. Campbell became a judo expert and was a member of the U.S. judo team in the 1964 Olympic Games in Tokyo. During the late 1960's and the 1970's, he built a successful business as a jewelry designer and jewelry maker and became a resident of Colorado. Campbell served in the Colorado House of Representatives from 1983 until 1986, when he was elected to the U.S. House of Representatives. He won reelection to the U.S. House in 1988 and 1990. In 1992, Campbell was elected to the United States Senate. He became the first American Indian since the late 1920's to hold a U.S. Senate seat.

Tantoo Cardinal is a Canadian-born member of the Métis. She has appeared in the films, Black Robe and Legends of the Fall and the television movies Lakota Woman and Tecumseh.

Charles Curtis, whose mother was a full-blooded member of the Kaw tribe, was elected vice president of the United States in 1929. He served under President Herbert Hoover from March 4, 1929 to March 3, 1933. He had served in the U.S. House of Representatives from 1893 to 1907 and in the U.S. Senate from 1907 to 1913 and 1915 to 1929 before becoming vice president.

Ada Deer was appointed the first female Assistant Secretary of the Interior for Indian Affairs in 1993. She was born on a Menominee reservation in 1935 in northern Wisconsin. She was the first member of

her tribe to graduate from the University of Wisconsin. She was also the first American Indian to earn a master's degree from the School of Social Work at Columbia University.

During the 1970s, Ada returned to her reservation to help the Menominee tribe avoid termination of federal money. She lobbied Congress and rallied supporters. On December 22, 1973, President Nixon signed the Menominee Restoration Act! Her people were saved! It was the first time Congress reversed itself on a specific matter of Indian policy.

Ada became the tribal chairperson, began lecturing, served on national boards, worked for human rights, and ran for political office in Wisconsin. She was a delegate to the Democratic National convention in 1984. As Assistant Secretary of the Interior for Indian Affairs, Ada helped recognize more than 200 Alaska native villages and reorganized the Bureau for Indian Affairs. She resigned her position in 1997 and began teaching American Indian Studies at the University of Wisconsin.

Louise Erdrich writes stories about three generations of Indians living in North Dakota in best-sellers such as Love Medicine and Track.

Harry Fonseca is best known for his humorous paintings of Coyote, a character in many Native American myths whose misadventures traditionally taught Indians lessons about good and bad behavior.

Graham Greene was nominated for an Academy Award for his performance as Kicking Bird in Dances with Wolves.

Joy Harjo is an acclaimed poet whose books include She Had Some Horses and In Mad Love and War. With her band Poetic Justice, she also performs songs based on her poems.

Ira Hayes belonged to the Pima Nation. He bravely fought for the United States and the Allied Forces during World War II. Hayes was one of six brave U.S. Marines to raise the American flag during heavy Japanese gunfire on Iwo Jima, an island in the Pacific Ocean. Despite his heroic acts, Ira returned home to discrimination, hatred, and prejudice.

John Bennett Herrington, mission specialist astronaut and U.S. Navy commander, became the first American Indian in space on

November 23, 2002 on flight STS-133 aboard the space shuttle Endeavor. He flew to the International Space Station from NASA's Kennedy Space Center in Cape Canaveral, Florida. John is a registered member of the Chickasaw Nation, so he carried a Chickasaw Nation flag with him.

During the eleven-day expedition, John also became the first American Indian to walk in space. NASA chose John to become an astronaut in 1996. He has logged more than 3,300 flight hours in more than 30 different types of aircraft! John is a naval aviator, naval test pilot, and holds a masters degree in aeronautical engineering from the U.S. Naval Postgraduate School. John is also a Sequoyah Fellow with the American Indian Science and Engineering Society.

Philip Johnston, a Navajo engineer, initiated the Navajo Code Talkers during World War II. After the attack on Pearl Harbor, the U.S. Marines realized that their Japanese enemies had broken U.S. military codes. The Marines still needed to send secret messages about war strategies, but they didn't want the Japanese to read them. They needed a new code.

Philip suggested that Navajo soldiers send the messages in their native language! The Marines recruited 29 young Navajo men to create the code. The work of these Navajo "Code Talkers" saved thousands of lives and ultimately helped win the war. The code worked so well that eventually more than 400 Navajo Code Talkers were recruited to keep the process going. Since the code was so ideal, it remained classified for 23 years after the war ended.

On July 26, 2001, President George W. Bush awarded the Congressional Gold Medal to the 29 original Navajo Code Talkers for their success and courage, though only five men from this group are still alive. The 400 recruited Navajo Code Talkers were awarded silver medals later that year.

Winona LaDuke ran for U.S. vice president in 2000 with Ralph Nader, who ran for president. She also ran for U.S. vice president in 1996. At the age of 18, she spoke in front of the United Nations about Indian issues and since has become known as a voice for American Indian concerns throughout the United States and internationally. In 1989, LaDuke won the International Reebok Human Rights Award. Time Magazine named her one of the "50 Leaders for the Future" in 1995.

Chief Arvol Looking Horse is a 19th generation keeper of the Original Sacred White Buffalo Calf Pipe of the Lakota, Dakota, and Nakota Nations of the Sioux. He committed his life to working for freedom, peace, and the cultural revival and healing of his people. Chief Arvol worked with World Peace and Prayer Day and his Wolakota Foundation.

Wilma Mankiller was born in Oklahoma in 1945. She was the first woman elected Principal Chief of the Cherokee Nation, which numbers about 139,000 people, after serving as deputy chief in 1983. She worked to improve health care, education, adult literacy, community self-help programs, financial empowerment, and tribal government. Wilma is also a civil rights activist, government lobbyist, and women's rights activist.

Russell Means is active in the Colorado chapter of the American Indian Movement (AIM). He ran for president on the Libertarian Party ticket in 1987.

N. Scott Momaday Ph.D., Kiowa Indian, is a poet, novelist, playwright, storyteller, artist, and a professor of English and American literature. In 1969, he won a Pulitzer Prize for House Made of Dawn. Momaday is a member of the famous Kiowa Gourd Dance Society.

Shelley Niro is a photographer and filmmaker. She uses playful self-portraits to explore the world of modern Native American women.

Leonard Peltier is an activist belonging to the American Indian Movement (AIM). He was convicted in 1976 of murdering two FBI agents on South Dakota's Pine Ridge Indian Reservation. He was sentenced to two consecutive life terms in prison.

    Many people around the world believe that Peltier is innocent. Seeing him as a political prisoner of the U.S. government, Peltier's supporters have spent more than 25 years campaigning for his case to be reexamined.

Earl Old Person, the current Chief of the Blackfeet Nation, was honored by the Montana chapter of the American Civil Liberties Union (ACLU) with its most prestigious award, the Jeannette Rankin Civil Liberties Award. Chief Old Person is one of the most highly esteemed and honored tribal leaders in Montana and the nation, having met with and been acknowledged by all U.S. Presidents from Eisenhower through

Clinton, the English Royal Family and Canadian Prime Ministers. He became Chief of the Blackfeet Nation, a lifetime appointment, in July of 1978.

Steve Reevis is a famous American Indian actor from the Blackfeet Nation reservation near Browning, Montana. He has acted for television and played roles in several films. Some of his film credits are Fargo, Geronimo: An American Legend, Dances with Wolves, The Missing, The Outfitters, Last of the Dogmen, Wild Bill, and Posse.

Katherine Siva Saubel, born in 1920, dedicated her life to the preservation of the language and culture of her people. As a young Cahuilla Indian girl, she grew up in a poor family on a reservation in Southern California. She was not allowed to speak her native language or disagree with how her people were portrayed in the history lessons. She became the first Indian girl to graduate from Palm Springs High School, and later earned scholarships to study anthropology.

In 1964, she and others founded the Malki Museum at the Morongo Reservation, the first Native American museum created and managed by Native Americans. She has helped write many books on language and culture, including Kunvachmal: A Cahuilla Tale.

Leslie Marmon Silko is the author of Ceremony and other novels. She often retells traditional Pueblo stories in her own words.

Jaune Quick-to-See Smith is a famous painter who uses her art to protest the mistreatment of Indian peoples in the past and present.

Maria Tallchief, born in 1925, is perhaps the most technically accomplished ballerina in American history. In the Ballet Russe de Monte Carlo, she danced in several major productions, including Swan Lake and The Nutcracker.

After Maria married her choreographer George Balanchine in 1946, the couple formed what eventually became the New York City Ballet. Maria spent 18 years there and served as prima ballerina for many years. She retired in 1965, but later founded the Chicago City Ballet in 1980.

Marie promoted Native American culture and contributions to the arts during her entire career. In 1953, the State of Oklahoma honored Maria with the name Wa-Xthe-Thomba, which meant "Woman of Two Worlds," to celebrate her dance career and Native American heritage.

Jim Thorpe was one of the greatest all-around athletes in history. He became an outstanding college and professional football player and won fame as an Olympic track and field champion. Thorpe also played major league baseball.

One of Thorpe's greatest athletic achievements occurred during the 1912 Olympic Games. He became the first athlete to win both the pentathlon and the decathlon. However, a short time later the Olympic committee took away Thorpe's medals. They said that because he had played baseball for a small salary, he was not eligible to compete in the games. At that time, only amateur athletes were allowed to compete.

Thorpe began his professional football career in 1915 and played on seven teams during the next 15 years. Thorpe helped establish professional football as a popular sport. In 1920, Thorpe became the first president of the American Professional Football Association, now known as the National Football League.

Thorpe died in 1953 and was buried in the Pennsylvania town of Mauch Chunk. The town was renamed Jim Thorpe in his honor! In 1982, the International Olympic Committee restored Thorpe's gold medals and added his name to the list of 1912 Olympic champions. In 1998, the United States Postal Service issued a commemorative stamp with his picture on it!

Annie Dodge Wauneka was born into a Navajo Nation hogan in 1910. Her wealthy father raised her and taught her Navajo history and culture. In 1918, an influenza epidemic struck her reservation. Thousands died, including many of Annie's Navajo classmates. Since Annie only suffered a mild case, she cared for the others. She later studied public health and worked to change health and sanitation standards among her fellow Navajo Indians.

In 1951, Annie became the second woman elected to the Tribal Council. She fought against tuberculosis and worked on several other health issues during her three terms in office. She even wrote a dictionary to translate English words into the Navajo language for modern medical techniques. She showed her people how modern medicine could help improve Navajo health on weekly radio broadcasts.

Annie also helped advise the U.S. Surgeon General and the U.S. Public Health Service. In 1963, she became the first Native American to receive the Presidential Medal of Freedom. Ladies' Home Journal even

chose her to be a Woman of the Year in 1976. In 1984, the Navajo Council designated her "The Legendary Mother of the Navajo Nation." She died in 1997.

John Woodenlegs, Sr. lectured across America about Northern Cheyenne history and culture. Under his leadership, Northern Cheyenne tribal members who wished to sell their land were required to offer the land first to the tribe before offering it to an outside buyer.

President Lyndon Johnson appointed him as the only Indian member of the National Advisory Commission of Rural Poverty.

He was the first Native American every given an honorary degree from the University of Montana. He received a Doctorate of Humane Letters in 1978 in Missoula. He was still teaching classes at Chief Dull Knife College at the time of his death in 1981.

Native Americans of Yesterday

Native American people flourished before non-Indians came to North America. Native American tribes had many similarities but also had their differences. There were millions of Native Americans before the first Europeans came to America. Europeans brought new weapons and diseases that killed many Native Americans.

Sometimes, Native American tribes went to war with each other, but sadly some Indians joined the non-Indians to fight other tribes. It wasn't until late in the 1800s and early in the 1900s that many leaders of Native American nations began to try and unite the tribes to work together to save their land.

The Native Americans of yesterday can teach us a lot today!

"They made us many promises, more than I can remember, but they never kept but one; they promised to take our land, and they took it."
—Unidentified Old Lakota

"No white person or persons shall be permitted to settle upon or occupy any portion of the territory, or without the consent of the Indians to pass through the same." —Treaty of 1868

Attakullakulla was a Cherokee chief in the 1700s during the time of war between the Cherokee Nation and the American Colonies.

Lewis Bennett "Deerfoot," who lived from 1828 to 1897, was an amazing long-distance runner. He practiced constantly during his youthful days with the Snipe Clan of the Seneca Indians. He did so well at the physical training tests, a tribal tradition carried out at his Cattaragus Reservation in New York State, that people began spreading a legend about him. They said that a horse had died of exhaustion after trying to outrun Lewis, who had outpaced the animal by more than thirty miles! Even though this story may not have been true, Lewis had developed a reputation as an athlete and soon began to run professionally (for pay).

In 1861, Lewis competed in England with the best runners of the British Isles. Though he lost the first race, he later began to win on a regular basis. In 1863, Lewis set records for his ten and twelve-mile runs, records that remained unbroken well into the twentieth century. Lewis loved to show his fans that he wasn't ashamed of his American Indian heritage. He wore wolfskin clothes and a feathered headband while running his races!

Black Elk was born in 1863 along the Little Powder River in northeast Wyoming. He was a member of the Oglala Lakota (Sioux). At the age of 13 Black Elk participated in the Battle of Little Bighorn. His family traveled with Crazy Horse, a distant cousin. From 1886-1889, Black Elk traveled the eastern United States and Europe with Buffalo Bill Cody's Wild West Show. They performed for Queen Victoria in England.

In 1931, the Nebraska poet John G. Neihardt recorded Black Elk's oral history. This account was first published in 1932 as Black Elk Speaks: The Life Story of a Holy Man of the Oglala Sioux. Neihardt met with Black Elk again in 1944, recording the history of the Lakota from creation to the time of contact with non-Indians, which appears in The

Sixth Grandfather, edited by Raymond J. De Maillie and published in 1984. Black Elk also acted as an informant for a book called The Sacred Pipe by Joseph Epes Brown. This book is about Lakota ritual and religion.

Black Hawk "Makataimeshekiakiak" was a Sauk war chief who lived between 1767 and 1838. He was born near Rock Island, Illinois in the Mississippi River. He refused to abide by the Treaty of St. Louis, which required the Sauk and Fox tribes to give up all their land claims east of the Mississippi. During the War of 1812, Black Hawk fought for the British under famous Shawnee leader Tecumseh.

In 1832, he led 200 warriors and their families back across the Mississippi River, but he got no help from neighboring tribes during the Black Hawk War. At Bad Axe River in Wisconsin, his band of Indians was outnumbered and Black Hawk was taken prisoner. President Andrew Jackson ordered him to come east the next year, and the dignified Sauk chief became a celebrity. His Autobiography was published in 1833 and became an American classic.

Black Kettle was a Southern Cheyenne chief who, despite broken promises and attacks on his own life, was regarded as a great leader with a unique vision that mainstream America and the plains Indians could live together. In 1868, a white flag was flying above the chief's own tepee. Black Kettle's village was well within the boundaries of the Cheyenne reservation. However, U.S. troops charged, and "both the chief and his wife fell at the river bank riddled with bullets," one witness reported.

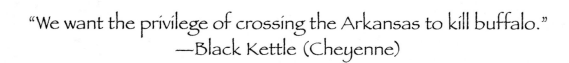

"We want the privilege of crossing the Arkansas to kill buffalo."
—Black Kettle (Cheyenne)

Billy Bowlegs was part of a ruling Seminole family and became a primary leader during the second Seminole War (1835–1842). For many years, he negotiated to keep his people from moving to Indian Territory (present-day Oklahoma). Finally he agreed to move to the reservation. In 1861, after the beginning of the Civil War, he fought to protect his home from the Confederate States. Billy Bowlegs became a captain in the Union Army's First Indian Regiment. He died in 1864.

Cochise led Apache warriors in raids on non-Indian travelers along the Butterfield Trail and on settlements. He was a master at hit-and-run tactics and was feared throughout southern Arizona. Cochise and his warriors had a hideout called the "Stronghold" in the Dragoon Mountains. For ten years they met there to plan attacks on non-Indians. In the fall of 1872, Cochise and his band of Apaches agreed to live peacefully on a reservation.

"You must speak straight so that your words may go as sunlight to our hearts." —Cochise (Apache)

Mangus Colorado was the leader of the Bendonkohe tribe of Apaches to which the famous warrior Geronimo belonged. American gold miners tricked Mangus into attending a peace conference in 1863. After traveling to their settlement with half of his tribe, the miners murdered them all. His son, Mangus, later became chief of the Bendonkohe Tribe.

Crazy Horse was called "Curly" as a child. It was only after he proved himself in battle did his father, also called Crazy Horse, give him his name. As a young man, Crazy Horse had a dream that one day he would be a great warrior. He proved himself in battle many times.

In 1876, Crazy Horse joined Sitting Bull and thousands of Sioux and Cheyenne warriors at the Battle of Little Bighorn. Crazy Horse was promised a reservation for his people if they would surrender, so he did. In 1877, Crazy Horse was arrested. He was killed while imprisoned at Fort Robinson.

"One does not sell the earth upon which the people walk." —Crazy Horse (Lakota)

Private Pierre Cruzatte was part French and part Omaha Indian. He is best known for helping Lewis and Clark explore the Louisiana Purchase. He was a small man, and only had one eye. An expert riverman, he was assigned to the crucial position of bowman in the

keelboat for his ability to spot the slack water eddies that would assist in advancing the boats upstream.

During the return journey, while elk hunting, Cruzatte accidentally shot Lewis in the leg. Cruzatte admitted it was an accident. Lewis was hurt but forgave the accident. Clark treated and dressed the wounds with medicine that they carried. Lewis was made comfortable but suffered a very painful healing process.

Cruzatte often entertained the explorers with his fiddle-playing. In the winter of 1804–1805, while they camped at Fort Mandan, Cruzatte's fiddle warmed their simple holiday celebrations. On New Year's Day 1805, Cruzatte and 17 others carried a fiddle and a tambourine across the river to the Mandan Indian village, entertaining the villagers with their singing, dancing and frolicking. This scene was repeated often along the way to the Pacific.

Cruzatte was also a valuable interpreter and knew sign language that helped Lewis and Clark negotiate through territory unknown and untraveled by the white man.

De-Ka-Nah-Wi-Da, known as "The Great Peacemaker," and Hiawatha formed Haudenosaunee, which means "People of the Long House." This Iroquois confederation is now more than five centuries old!

Dragging Canoe was born about 1732. In July 1776, Chief Dragging Canoe headed a force of 700 Cherokee and attacked two U.S. held forts in North Carolina: Eaton's Station and Fort Watauga. He is also remembered for his courageous "Battle of the Bluffs" campaign to save his beloved homelands of the Cumberland Valley. Dragging Canoe died on March 1, 1792 in Lookout Town, Tennessee.

Dull Knife was a war chief in the Plains Indian Wars. Dull Knife was one of the signers of the Fort Laramie Treaty of 1868. He and his warriors joined the Lakota (Sioux) in the War for the Black Hills of 1876–1877. Dull Knife was also a leader in the flight of the Northern Cheyenne. The Cheyenne were forced to move from their home in northern Wyoming and southern Montana to Indian Territory (present-day Oklahoma). Dull Knife unsuccessfully tried to lead a group of 300 Cheyenne Indians to their back to their home. In 1884, a year after Dull Knife's death, the Northern Cheyenne were granted the Tongue River Reservation in Montana.

Logan Fontenelle was a well-known chief of the Omaha tribe. He was born at Fort Atkinson in 1825. Fontenelle was the son of a French

fur trader and an Omaha Indian woman. After receiving his education in Saint Louis, he returned to Bellevue, where he was an interpreter for the United States Government from 1840 to 1853.

Although he was not a chief by blood, he was elected principal chief of the tribe in 1853 at the time that the transfer of the tribe to its northeast Nebraska reservation was being negotiated. He played an important part in the signing of the Treaty of 1854 which gave all of the Omaha Indian land to the government. Fontenelle was respected by members of his tribe and by the whites. While he maintained absolute control over the Omaha, he promoted education and agriculture.

Many Nebraska landmarks have been named for Logan Fontenelle, including a town (spelled "Fontanelle") in Washington County; Fontenelle Forest north of Bellevue; and parks, schools, streets, and public housing in eastern Nebraska.

El Mocho was born among the Apache, but was captured by the Tonkawa and taken to their homeland in central Texas. Demonstrating his courage to his captors, he soon earned his freedom. He bore his Spanish name because he had lost his right ear in a fight with the Osage. El Mocho means the cropped one. In 1782, hoping to unite the Tonkawa and Apache against the Spanish, he called a council attended by more than 4,000. Fearing his power, the Spanish hunted him, managing to kill him two years after his great council.

Gall of the Hunkpapa Sioux was born around 1840. He fought with Sitting Bull and Crazy Horse. Gall helped with battle strategy plans. These three Indian leaders led the Indian attack at the Battle Of The Little Bighorn. He was one of the greatest Hunkpapa Sioux chieftains in history.

After Gall stole some ponies, one hundred soldiers were sent to his village to arrest him in the middle of the night. They shot at him as soon as he stepped outside his tepee. When he tried to escape, they beat him until they thought he was dead and left his body in the snow. He actually wasn't dead, just badly wounded. He made his way to a friend's lodge twenty miles away. Gall's friend nursed his wounds, but he died later in 1894.

"If we make peace, you will not hold it." —Gall (Lakota)

Geronimo was born in Arizona in 1829. He played hide-and-seek with the other children, pretended to be a brave warrior, and played with his dogs and ponies. As an older boy, he helped plant crops and hunt for food. Geronimo entered the council of the warriors at age 17. He married and raised three children. Geronimo's father died when he was a young boy. His mother chose to live with Geronimo instead of remarrying.

In 1858, Mexican troops attacked the Apache camp. They destroyed supplies, killed the few guards, stole ponies and weapons, and killed most of the women and children. Geronimo's mother, wife, and three children were all massacred.

Geronimo burned everything his wife, children, and mother had owned. He vowed revenge on the Mexican troops. Geronimo and Apache warriors raided Mexican settlements many times. Enemies sometimes attacked the tribe as well. Many people died, on both sides.

Then the Apache met the Americans. The Apache tried to befriend the Americans, and U.S. officers asked to meet with their leaders. When the Indians entered a tent in the fort to meet, they were attacked by surprise! The chief escaped, but many warriors were killed. Geronimo never trusted another American.

In 1863, an American settlement offered peace and supplies to the Apache in 1863. Geronimo was suspicious, but Chief Mangus traveled there with half of the tribe. The chief never returned. The warriors heard they had all been murdered. Geronimo was made chief. American troops began to fight the remaining Apache warriors, who were now without many weapons or supplies. Many battles took place. Geronimo was jailed, then released. The U.S. forced him to work hard many years in the Southeast.

Geronimo survived eight battle wounds. He was shot in the right knee, left forearm, left side, back, and the outside corner of his left eye. He was also wounded by a sword and hit on the head with a musket. He later became a Christian, attended the St. Louis World's Fair and President Theodore Roosevelt's inauguration ceremony, and helped write a book about his life. Geronimo died in 1909.

Iron Tail fought in the War for the Black Hills of 1876–1877 and was an aide to fellow Lakota (Sioux) Sitting Bull at Little Bighorn. He later joined Buffalo Bill Cody's Wild West Show and accompanied it to Europe in 1889. The artist James Fraser used Iron Tail, along with two other Native Americans, as models for the "buffalo" or "Indian head" nickel.

"There is one God looking down upon us all." Geronimo (Apache)

Ignacio helped guide his people through one of the most difficult periods of Ute history. Born in 1828, Chief Ignacio witnessed the increasing influx of whites into Colorado, saw Ute lands diminish after each successive treaty with the United States government, and watched his people starve as their supply of game dwindled. In 1880, Chief Ignacio and other Utes traveled to Washington D.C. to negotiate a treaty that would result in the removal of the White River and Tabeguache Utes from Colorado to the Uintah Basin in present day Utah. Chief Ouray died at age 47 shortly after this trip. Chief Ignacio served as a leader of the Weeminuche band for eighty-five years.

Chief Joseph (Hinmaton-Yalaktit) is regarded as one of the greatest of Indian strategists. He was part of the last phase of the Indian Wars in the West. Chief Joseph became chief of the Nez Perce after his father died in 1873. He refused to recognize an 1863 agreement that gave away their lands and forced them to live on a reservation in Idaho. Once Chief Joseph realized, however, that his two hundred warriors were no match for the United States Army, he planned an escape with women and children to Canada. In 1877 he led a brilliant retreat more than a thousand miles through Montana and Idaho, while enduring one army and defeating another. After battle lasting five days, he finally surrendered. Chief Joseph and his people were only thirty miles from safety and the Canadian border. After that, Chief Joseph devoted his live to helping his people learn peaceful ways.

"I have fought; but from where the sun now stands I will fight no more forever." —Chief Joseph of the Nez Perce

Susette La Flesche was born to Omaha Chief Joseph La Flesche in 1854. She was the first Native American lecturer and the first published Native American artist and writer. The English translation of her Native American name, Inshta Theumba, meant "Bright Eyes." She taught on her reservation after finishing college. Then in 1879, Susette lectured with Omaha Herald journalist Thomas Tibbles around the country about how the Ponca Indians had been mistreated. More than one third of the group had died during relocation to unfamiliar lands. By talking with powerful Easterners, Susette helped the Dawes Act get approved in 1887. This progressive law helped tribes. She later married Tibbles, continued to lecture in America and England, and began writing for several magazines and newspapers. She also anonymously edited Ploughed Under, The Story of an Indian Chief. Susette died in 1903.

Handsome Lake experiences several visions while lying on his deathbed in 1799. He said these visions were messages from the Creator for the Iroquois Indians. After he recovered from the illness, Handsome Lake preached a series of messages to the Seneca of the Iroquois tribe. These words were later known as the Code of Handsome Lake.

Little Crow was a Santee Sioux chief. In 1851 he signed a treaty with the federal government giving up almost all his people's territory in Minnesota. Although he was not happy with the agreement, he kept his promise for many years. In 1862, other members of his tribal council were upset at the delay of federal payments to the Sioux. They convinced Little Crow to attack white settlements. More than a thousand whites were killed and many farms were destroyed. Little Crow fled to Canada, but soon returned to Minnesota. In 1863, he was killed by a settler while looking for food in a forest outside of St. Paul.

Mountain Chief, great Blackfeet leader of the late 1800s, who refused to compromise or cooperate with the U.S. government.

Naiche, the youngest son of Apache Chief Cochise, fought with a small band of runaway Apaches that included Geronimo, Chappo (Geronimo's son), Fun, Cayetano, Chihuahua, Perico (Geronimo's brother) and others. They battled against thousands of American troops for more than two years. When Naiche was captured with Geronimo, they were sent to Florida as military prisoners.

Ohiyesa [Dr. Charles Alexander Eastman], a Santee Sioux Indian, was raised in traditional Indian ways. He graduated from Dartmouth College, New Hampshire, in 1887, and studied medicine at Boston University. After his education, he became a famous author.

Osceola "Black Drink" was never a hereditary or elected chief, but he bravely led the Seminole Indians against relocation efforts by the U.S. government. In 1835 he was asked to sign a treaty that would move his people west of the Mississippi. He slammed his knife into the paper, giving a direct answer. The seven-year Second Seminole War began soon afterward. Osceola was tricked into capture in 1837 while carrying a white truce flag. He was thrown into prison at Fort Moultrie, South Carolina. He later died of malaria.

Oskanondonha was a leader of the Oneida Nation. He became a great hero of the Revolutionary War. Oskanondonha was born in 1710 and lived for 106 years.

Ouray is considered one of the Ute's greatest leaders. He led the Southern Ute tribe during the mid-1800s. He learned Spanish and English as well as several Indian languages, which were useful in negotiations. In 1863 he helped negotiate a treaty with the federal government in which the Ute ceded all lands east of the Continental Divide. For his services, Ouray received an annuity of $1,000. Because of special favors he received from the whites, Ouray was forced to kill at least five Ute in various attempts on his life.

Ely Parker was a Seneca Indian with legal training. He was admitted to the military only after Ulysses Grant intervened. Ely Parker made history by writing out the terms of the final Confederate surrender. Later, under Grant's presidency, Parker made history again as head of the federal commission on Indian affairs. Robert E. Lee once mistook Parker for a black man, but corrected himself at Appomattox saying, "I am glad to see one real American here."

Quanah Parker Quanah, meaning "fragment," was born about 1850, son of Commanche Chief Peta Nocona and Cynthia Ann Parker, a white girl taken captive during an Indian raid. He was the last Chief of the Comanche Nation and never lost a battle to the white man. He was never captured by the Army, but decided to surrender and lead his tribe into the white man's culture, only when he saw that there was no alternative.

Quanah learned English, became a reservation judge, lobbied Congress, and pleaded the cause of the Comanche nation. Among his friends were cattleman Charles Goodnight and President Theodore Roosevelt.

Susan La Flesche Picotte distinguished herself by becoming the first Native American woman ever to earn a

medical degree and work as a practicing M.D. After completing her studies and earning her degree, Susan returned to Nebraska as a government physician. She rode on horseback from reservation to reservation, from family to family, treating the sick. It is said that, by the time of her death, she had treated every member of the Omaha Nation.

After a time, she married and settled in Bancroft, Nebraska where she had a private practice treating both Native and white patients. Flesche married in the summer of 1894 and added her husband's last name, Picotte, to her own. She adopted Christianity, and became a missionary of the Omaha Blackbird Hills Presbyterian Church. She moved to the newly established town of Walthill and founded a hospital there.

Susan went on to be a leading citizen of Walthill, and headed a delegation to Washington, D.C. to fight against the sale of liquor in Nebraska. She was so successful in her endeavors that a covenant was placed in land sale documents of that time prohibiting the possession of liquor on any land purchased from the Omaha.

Peter Perkins Pitchlynn, also known as Hat-choo-tuck-nee "The Snapping Turtle," was born at Hushookwa village in Mississippi. He was the son of a white interpreter and a Choctaw Indian woman from an influential family. He decided that he needed an Indian education and an American education. He traveled to a non-Indian school 200 miles away to learn for one semester. He later graduated from Nashville University.

Peter was elected to the Choctaw National Council in the 1820s. Part of his duties included helping choose new lands for his tribe when they were relocated west of the Mississippi. He signed the Treaty of Dancing Rabbit Creek, then helped reorganize his tribe in their new home. He supported five new English-language schools a ban on alcohol, and often traveled to Washington, D.C. on behalf of his people. Peter was elected principal chief in 1864. Before he died in 1881, Peter, who enjoyed writing poetry and reading English literature, met famous author Charles Dickens.

Pocahontas was born in 1596 near present-day Jamestown, Virginia. Her mother died during birth, so her father, Chief Powhatan, raised her in the Chickahominy tribe. She was her father's favorite child. She could run, hunt, and shoot arrows with the boys.

Some English settlers sailed to America, which they called the New World, when Pocahontas was twelve years old. They built a settlement

22

called Jamestown near her village. Her tribe helped the colonists survive by teaching them about the land. When Captain James Smith of Jamestown visited Chief Powhatan and his tribe, he was sentenced to death. According to legend, Pocahontas begged that his life be spared. He was set free.

A few years later, Pocahontas visited Jamestown. She wanted to learn about the English and their strange ways. The colonists liked her. Then the Indians and colonists began to distrust each other. In 1613, the colonists kidnapped Pocahontas! She lived with the deputy governor and his wife, learned English, and became the first Indian to convert to Christianity. Pocahontas married an English tobacco farmer named John Rolfe the next year. Their marriage helped heal relations between the Indians and the colonists. Peace lasted for about eight years.

In 1616, John and Pocahontas traveled back to England to encourage more people to come to America. Pocahontas met many people, including Queen Anne. The next year, the Rolfes prepared to sail home so John could take care of his tobacco farm. Before the ship left, Pocahontas became ill. She died at age 21 and was buried in England.

Pontiac believed that if the Indian tribes united and won French support, they could drive the British from the Great Lakes region. Pontiac and other Native American allies of the French were upset at the outcome of the French and Indian War. The Treaty of Paris ceded Indian lands west of the Appalachians to the British. In 1763, he led the Pontiac Rebellion that captured British forts in present-day Ohio, Michigan, Indiana, Pennsylvania, and Wisconsin.

In 1765, he agreed to a peace pact and signed a treaty at Oswego in 1766. In 1769 another Indian (probably paid by the British who still feared his influence) killed Pontiac.

Chief Powhatan ruled more than 9,000 Indians in eastern Virginia. The Indians respected and obeyed Chief Powhatan. They paid him taxes and he took care of them. He had between 40 and 50 bodyguards. He had more than 100 wives and dozens of children. Pocahontas was his favorite.

When strange settlers from foreign lands like Spain and France and England came, Chief Powhatan was worried. The new settlers brought diseases like smallpox, influenza, measles, and plagues. The Indians had never been exposed to these germs before and many died. Chief Powhatan did not trust the Europeans. He was not happy to find

23

out that they wanted to stay and not just trade. Though he did not declare war, he allowed his warriors to attack the colonists.

Chief Powhatan wanted guns, like the Europeans had, to defend his people better. When the colonists refused his request, some Powhatan Indians raided the colonial Jamestown settlement and stole them. The colonists then kidnapped Chief Powhatan's daughter, Pocahontas. He was surprised and saddened when she quickly adapted to the European culture and did not come home. Her marriage to a colonist inspired peace between the Indians and the colonists, but it ended in 1618 when Chief Powhatan died.

Pushmataha negotiated several treaties with the United States and led Choctaws in support of the Americans during the War of 1812. In April 2001, a new Pushmataha portrait was unveiled to hang in the Hall of Fame of the State of Mississippi in the Old Capitol Museum in Jackson, Mississippi. Pushmataha is buried in the Congressional Cemetery in Washington, D.C.

"We do not take up the warpath without a just cause and honest purpose." —Pushmataha (Choctaw)

General Stand Waite, a full-blooded Cherokee chief, was the only Native American Indian to become a Brigadier General (Union or Confederacy) during the U.S. Civil War. He led the Cherokee Mounted Rifles party into battle for the Confederacy and was the last general to surrender to the Union.

Red Cloud is considered to be one of the greatest warriors and chiefs of the Oglala Sioux. He had an important ability for telling tales in a lively and convincing manner. Although he was known for his successfulness on the battlefield, his speaking ability helped him gain the loyalty of thousands of warriors. Red Cloud's ability to fight as well as his determination to protect his people earned him a reputation as a bold and spirited fighter.

Red Cloud was in a group of Indians which went to Washington in 1870. His actions and speech indicated that he had changed his ideas about war and was an advocate of peace. His trip was called Red Cloud's Peace Crusade. He was a guest of President

Ulysses S. Grant in the White House, and then went to New York, where he made a speech in front of a packed crowd.

The front page story in the New York Times of June 17, 1870 told a story of how every person in the audience was affected by Red Cloud's remarkable speech. Red Cloud told the audience that all he wanted was "right and justice."

"We, too, have children, and we wish to bring them up well."
—Red Cloud (Lakota)

Major Ridge was born about 1770 in present-day Tennessee. He was educated by relatives and neighbors and elected to the Cherokee Council when 21. As a young man, he participated in raids on non-Indian settlers.

The Ridge earned the title "Major" during the Creek War of 1813–1814 as an ally of General Andrew Jackson. He was a signer of the Treaty of Echota in 1835 and, after relocation to the Indian Territory (present-day Oklahoma) he was killed by others who disagreed with the treaty.

John Ross was the first and only elected Chief of the Cherokee Nation from the time it was formed until his death in 1866. Although only one-eighth Cherokee, Ross played Native American games and kept his Indian ties. Early in his life he was postmaster in Rossville, Ga. and a clerk in a trading firm. The town he founded as Rossville Landing grew much larger than it's namesake as Chattanooga, Tennessee. Ross, one of the richest men in North Georgia before 1838 had a number of ventures including a 200-acre farm.

"Be peace our condition has been improved in the pursuit of civilized life."
—John Ross (Cherokee)

Sacagawea was born in a northern Shoshone village near the Lemhi River valley, presently Idaho. As a young girl, she was kidnapped by enemy Hidatsa Indians and taken to live by Knife River, presently North Dakota. Sacagawea was later sold to a French-Canadian fur trader named Toussaint Charbonneau.

Meriwether Lewis and William Clark hired the couple as interpreters and guides on their Western exploration expedition in 1805. Sacagawea gave birth to her first child, Jean Baptiste, on the journey. She taught the explorers land survival skills, showed them how to understand the rivers and landscapes, and helped the party find food and medicine in the wilderness. Sacagawea even helped save Clark's journals and records when his boat nearly capsized.

Sacagawea also served as Lewis and Clark's ambassador during meetings with other Indians. For example, she acquired supplies from her Shoshone relatives when Lewis and Clark were crossing the Continental Divide via the Bitterroot Mountains. In November of 1805, the expedition reached the shores of the Pacific Ocean, and Sacagawea saw the "great waters" for the first time.

Satanta, also known as Set'tainte and White Bear, was a Kiowa chief who tried to stop the Americans from destroying Kiowa tribal sovereignty. He used both diplomacy and warfare to meet this goal. When he stood trial with Ado-eete in Jacksboro, Texas for the Salt Creek Massacre, he became the first Indian chief forced to stand trial in a civil court.

"I love the land and the buffalo and will not part with it." Satanta (Kiowa)

Chief Seattle (Duwamish chief) delivered a famous speech in 1854 when representatives of the U.S. government came to the Northwest to try buying his people's lands and discuss reservations. "There was a time when our people covered the land as the waves of a wind-ruffled sea cover its shell paved floor, but that time long since passed away with the greatest of tribes that are now but a mournful memory..."

As a boy in 1792, he remembered seeing non-Indians first arrive in Puget Sound in what is now Washington state. He encouraged friendship and peace between them and the Indians. In 1852, the Puget Sound settlement was named Seattle after him. He married twice and had six children. Four of them died young.

In 1855, he reluctantly signed the Fort Elliot Treaty with Isaac Ingalls Stevens, the governor of Washington Territory, and agreed to allow his people to be relocated to a reservation. When the whites broke this treaty, the Yakama War (1855–56) broke out and many died.

Seattle still sought peace and led his people to the Port Madison Reservation to live. Seattle died in 1866.

Sequoyah was born in Tennessee among (Cherokee) Tsalagi warriors. His father was a white explorer. However his mother had descended from chiefs. She belonged to the old Red Paint Clan. Sequoyah loved drawing, woodworking, sports, storytelling, and working with silver.

Though Sequoyah's leg became lame as a youth in a hunting accident, he fought Creek Indians in the War of 1812. During this war, Sequoyah saw white soldiers sending and storing information on "talking leaves" or papers with words. Most Cherokee were illiterate because English was difficult to learn, and there was no written Cherokee language. He realized that the European settlers' ability to read and write gave them power over the Indians.

Sequoyah began to listen to Cherokees talking and looked for syllables that made up words. He drew a symbol for each sound on bark. After 12 years, Sequoyah chose 85 separate sounds and a character to represent each syllable. Sequoyah's alphabet was the first written Cherokee language!

No one understood Sequoyah's excitement. His wife even burned down his workshop! He decided to leave with his youngest daughter, Ahyokeh, for Arkansas to find acceptance among the Cherokee living there.

Sequoyah needed to teach his language to a student. He taught Ahyokeh! In 1821, Sequoyah demonstrated his language to the Cherokee council. From a great distance, he sent a written message to Ahyokeh. She read it correctly. The amazed council gave Sequoyah a medal and adopted his alphabet as the Cherokee language. The alphabet was easy to master. Students only had to learn the 85 syllables to read or write any word in the Cherokee language. Thanks to Sequoyah the Cherokee people quickly became literate.

Sitting Bull "Tatanka-Iyotanka" was born near present-day Bullhead, South Dakota to the Lakota (Sioux) tribe. His father was a respected chief. Sitting Bull killed his first bull at age ten and fought in his first battle four years later. He joined a raiding warrior society called the Strong Hearts.

In 1863, Sitting Bull first fought American soldiers. They were attacking a wide area of Indian Territory because of the Santee Rebellion in Minnesota. Sitting Bull's people had not joined in that

rebellion, but U.S. troops were still attacking them! Sitting Bull had no choice but to fight back. The Lakota Indians admired and trusted Sitting Bull. He was strong, brave, and wise. He was named chief of the Lakota nation. It was now his job to protect the people from harm.

In 1874, the Lakota were forced to defend their land when prospectors came to find gold. This led to the Great Sioux War. The United States tried to buy the Black Hills. When the Lakota refused to sell, the United States declared that all Lakota Indians who did not move to reservations would be enemies! Sitting Bull and his people stayed.

Cheyenne, Lakota, and Arapaho Indians offered prayers to the Great Spirit in a Sun Dance. American troops set up to attack the Indians. During the dance, Sitting Bull dreamed he saw soldiers falling into the Lakota camp from the sky. His vision inspired another chief named Crazy Horse, who attacked the U.S. troops by surprise with 500 warriors. The troops retreated, and the Indians moved into the Little Bighorn River valley. More Indians left reservations to join Sitting Bull. General George Custer and the Seventh Cavalry attacked the Indian army, but they were outnumbered. Every soldier in Custer's party died in the Battle of Little Bighorn.

The U.S. Army sent more troops to attack the tribes. Many Lakota chiefs surrendered, but Sitting Bull refused. Four years later, he was forced to give up because he could no longer feed his people since the buffalo were growing scarce. Sitting Bull was sent to Standing Rock Reservation. He was reunited with his tribe after being held prisoner for two years. Sitting Bull was paid $50 a week to ride once around the arena in Buffalo Bill's Wild West show. He soon could not tolerate white society and left.

In 1890, reservation police feared Sitting Bull might join a group of Indian rebels called the Ghost Dancers. During his arrest, Sitting Bull was shot dead. Before he died, Sitting Bull said, "I wish it to be remembered that I was the last man of my tribe to surrender my rifle."

"If a man loses anything and goes back and looks carefully for it he will find it, and that is what the Indians are doing now when they ask you to give them the things that were promised them in the past; and I do not consider that they should be treated like beasts, and that is the reason I have grown up with the feeling I have." —Sitting Bull (Lakota)

Squanto is thought to have been kidnapped by Thomas Hunt, captain of a ship under the overall command of John Smith in 1614, then taken to Europe, and sold into slavery. Eventually, he returned to New England with a man named Captain Thomas Dermer who hoped to colonize the area. Squanto had learned to speak English while in captivity and helped the pilgrims with fishing and planting corn. He also showed them how to catch herring and use them as fertilizer. Squanto helped make possible the first Thanksgiving feast in the autumn of 1621.

Standing Bear was born on the Ponca reservation in what is now Nebraska around 1834. He became a chief at an early age. In 1876 when the Ponca were told they were to be moved to Indian Territory (present-day Oklahoma), they sent ten chiefs with a United States agent to look over the land and its prospects. They were to make a decision for the Ponca tribe. The chiefs could not make a favorable report, and the tribe voted not to go to Indian Territory. The government then decided to force the Ponca to Indian Territory. So the Ponca left on foot for Indian Territory, escorted by the U.S. Army.

Standing Bear and thirty others tried to return to their home on the Niobrara. They were stopped on the Omaha Reservation and arrested on orders from the Secretary of Interior at Washington, D.C. During this time, their story appeared in the Omaha World-Herald.

In 1879 a United States District court case in Omaha led to a decision by Judge Elmer Dundy that native Americans are "persons within the meaning of the law" and have the rights of citizenship. The government tried to prove that an Indian was neither a person nor a citizen so couldn't bring suit against the government. On April 30, 1879 Judge Dundy stated that an Indian is a person within the law and that the Ponca were being held illegally. He set free Standing Bear and the Ponca. A government commission, appointed by President Rutherford B. Hayes, investigated and found the Ponca situation to be unjust. They arranged for the return of the Ponca from Indian Territory and allotted land to them along the Niobrara River.

Tecumseh ("Panther Crossing") was a great Shawnee Indian leader. He was born in 1768 in central Ohio to Pucksinwa, a warrior chief who died when Tecumseh was young. After his father's death, Tecumseh's mother moved south with her tribe. Tecumseh trained to become a warrior.

Tecumseh fought to keep his Shawnee lands. He refused to sign the Treaty of Greenville after the Battle of Fallen Timbers because he did not want his tribe to be relocated to northwestern Ohio. The elders did not know what to do. Tecumseh thought that the Indian tribes would be strongest if they banded together. He thought that if the Indians had a unified government, the Americans could not trick them one tribe at a time. Soon many tribes joined Tecumseh's cause. The American settlers grew alarmed.

While Tecumseh was away, his brother Tenskwatawa "The Prophet" decided to attack the white men. General William Henry Harrison set up troops near Prophetstown, and when Tenskwatawa led the men into battle, they were defeated. General Harrison burned down the town and all of Tecumseh's supplies.

Tecumseh fought for Great Britain in the War of 1812, hoping they would reward the Indians for military support by returning their lands. Thought he served bravely as a Brigadier General, Great Britain lost the war. With that defeat, Tecumseh lost hope in ever recovering the Shawnee lands. He died at the Battle of the Thames on October 5, 1813. He was buried in a secret location away from the battlefield.

"No tribe has the right to sell, even to each other, much less to strangers... sell a country! Why not sell the air, the great sea, as well as the earth?"
—Tecumseh (Shawnee)

Tenskwatawa was also known as "The Prophet." He was a brother to Techumseh, and both were Shawnee leaders who tried to unite Native Americans against whites during the early 1800s. William Henry Harrison defeated them near Tippecanoe in the Indiana Territory. This defeat opened up the Ohio River Valley to White settlement.

Chief Thundercloud was a member of the Blackfeet tribe and a U.S. Army scout for many Indian wars. Frederic Remington and John Singer Sargent, famous "Wild West" artists, often used Chief Thundercloud as a model for their paintings. His profile was even engraved on the last gold coins minted in the United States. Chief Thundercloud lived from 1856 to 1916.

Tichkematse (Squint Eyes) was an early employee of the Smithsonian Institution. He was a Cheyenne Indian who worked there between 1879 and 1881. Tichkematse was among a group of southern

Plains warriors who were held as prisoners of war by the United States government from 1875–1878. While imprisoned, he learned to speak English and to read and write. Upon release he attended school in Virginia for about a year. There he was trained in the preparation of bird and mammal specimens for study and display.

Chief Joseph Tonasket worked for peace after the McLoughlin Canyon battle in 1858, when a party of miners had been ambushed just south of present-day Tonasket, Washington. Chief Tonasket tried to persuade the Indians to return to the miners the land they had captured.

Tonasket, a town 25 miles south of the Canadian border, was named after the Okanogan Indian chief Joseph Tonasket. The inscription on his headstone reads, Chief Joseph Tonasket 1822–1891, "He proved himself a strong and able leader, and although his was not an inherited Chieftain-Chief, he was officially recognized as Chief of the Okanogan Indians in about the year 1858. His life was a series of accomplishments for his people."

James Vann made many changes to the Cherokee world during his life. He was the son of a Scottish trader and his Cherokee wife. Vann's father was among the first white traders in the Cherokee Nation. Vann's early recognition came because he was one of the few Cherokee who could read English. As a teenager he was called to read letters to the tribe from Tennessee Governor John Sevier.

In death Vann would have a major effect on Cherokee society. The society was structured around Cherokee women, not men. When a man married he became a member of his wife's clan. Property passed through a wife when a warrior died. Vann, in line with white law of the time, left his inheritance to his son Joseph. The tribal council gave some of the inheritance to his wives and other children, but Joseph got the bulk.

When he died, Vann was one of the richest men not only in the Cherokee Nation but in the United States. His beautiful home along the Federal Highway still bears his name, Vann House, and is a popular stop along North Georgia's Chieftains Trail.

Victorio was among the most feared and admired Indians in the Southwest. He was born into the Warm Springs Apache tribe in New Mexico. Victorio often led warriors on raids in Northern Mexico, Eastern Arizona, and Southwestern New Mexico. Victorio was a close friend of Geronimo and Naiche.

Sarah Winnemucca, born in 1842, was the daughter of Chief Winnemucca of the Paiutes, a tribe in Nevada and California. After losing some of her family in the Paiute War of 1860, Sarah decided she would work for peace. She became an interpreter at a U.S. Army camp, using language skills learned in a Catholic school.

In 1872, Sarah traveled with her tribe to the Malheur reservation. She became a U.S. Army scout. During the Bannock War, she bravely freed several captives, including her father, taken hostage by the Bannock Indians. Sarah gave more than 300 lectures in major eastern cities to tell others about how her tribe had been mistreated by dishonest Indian agents and exiled from their homelands. Though even President Rutherford Hayes and Interior Secretary Carl Schurz listened to her pleas, Sarah's people were never returned to their homelands. She wrote a book, Life Among the Piutes: Their Wrongs and Claims, in 1883 and later founded a school.

"Will you teach your children what we have taught our children? That the earth is our mother? What befalls the earth befalls all the sons of the earth. "This we know: the earth does not belong to man, man belongs to the earth. All things are connected like the blood that unites us all. Man did not weave the web of life, he is merely a strand in it. Whatever he does to the web, he does to himself. "One thing we know: our god is also your god. The earth is precious to him and to harm the earth is to heap contempt on its creator. "
—Chief Seattle

"Is it wrong for me to love my own? Is it wicked for me because my skin is red? Because I am Sioux? Because I was born where my father lived? Because I would die for my people and my country? God made me an Indian." —Chief Sitting Bull